THOSE
WHOM
GOD
CHOOSES

THOSE WHOM GOD CHOOSES

BY
BARBARA AND GREY VILLET

A STUDIO BOOK
THE VIKING PRESS
NEW YORK

Nihil obstat
Rt. Rev. Matthew P. Stapleton
Diocesan Censor

Imprimatur
✠ Richard Cardinal Cushing
Archbishop of Boston

December 21, 1965

First published in 1966 by The Viking Press, Inc.
625 Madison Avenue, New York, N.Y. 10022

Published simultaneously in Canada by
The Macmillan Company of Canada Limited

Library of Congress catalog card number: 66-15417
Printed by
Mondadori - Verona - Italy

Portions of this book first appeared in Life.

FOREWORD

In the last few years nuns have become a more common sight than they were in former times. Most of us can remember the days when they seemed to be relegated to their high, forbidding convents behind massive walls, seldom appearing in public, and busy about the many religious tasks that traditionally occupy religious women in the work of the Church. Now the various sisterhoods have become more visible, and many earlier restrictions on their activities have been modified so that we find them moving more and more among the people, bringing into the active world the influence of their holy lives.

Then, too, many people with little religious affiliation have come to know the nuns through fiction and the cinema; too often here, however, the picture of the nun is completely unrealistic, sometimes over-forbidding, sometimes over-saccharine. There is a real need to understand in some depth the vocation of the religious woman, to see the motives that bring a young woman to seek out this way of life and to appreciate the dedication that endures through all the years that follow. For most people, even Catholics who have known many religious, there is always an element of mystery about the convent and convent life and most especially about the young Christian girl who so generously gives herself to the Lord in this final and complete fashion.

We know, of course, that there is a mystery here, the mystery of God's grace, which transforms the human spirit and raises to the supernatural our finite efforts. But the vocation to the religious life is not just some act of sacrifice, some decision of self-abnegation, some withdrawal from the world; it is a positive act of love that embraces both God and man, a wide and deep commitment to the best that is in us. Unless we see it in terms that are joyful and unselfish, positive and productive, we do not understand it at all.

The pictures in these pages can help to give a real dimension to a world that is too often merely fascinating, or just incomprehensible, to modern man. From it the reader may catch some of the authentic spirit that has moved thousands upon thousands of young women, even in these easy and affluent times, to seek and find a full life in the service of the Lord. My hope is that these pages will encourage some to follow the religious life, but even more that they will stimulate a torrent of grateful prayers for all those who have accepted God's call and now labor in the vineyard of the Lord.

RICHARD CARDINAL CUSHING
Archbishop of Boston

THOSE
WHOM
GOD
CHOOSES

CHAPTER

I

Shrouded in long black robes, her face half hidden in the curve of her black veils, a nun seems an apparition of an age long dead. She is a mystifying anachronism, who has forsworn freedom, marriage, and motherhood to live by a rule and in a manner little changed since the Middle Ages. To some her rejection of the world marks her as one chosen by God to live a nearly perfect life. To others she seems an unnatural creature who has run from sex and reality to immolate herself in the harsh disciplines of the convent. To herself she is likely to appear more sinner than saint, an imperfect human being struggling to follow the divine will and listening for a voice that others do not hear.

The dialogue of self and soul that becomes a vocation usually begins early in a girl's life, culminating during adolescence with the romantic conviction that God has chosen her to serve Him in a special way. She attaches the emotions usually reserved for first love to the dream of becoming the Lord's handmaiden. Her feelings about entering the convent are not very different from those of a young woman about to be married. "All of them are going through an adolescent love affair with all the frills when they first come to us," said the Mistress of Postulants for the Missionary Society of Mary. "Later, as in marriage, they settle down and notice what the world is really like. But God has his compensations, and one of them is this romantic fling of the little ones. It gets them through what otherwise would be an almost impossible sacrifice. The fling is over and the true vocation starts to be settled on the day a girl looks back over the wall and sees a young woman her own age in pretty clothes wheeling a baby carriage past the convent. Then her heart sinks, and she knows what it is that

God is really asking of her. It's then she finds out if she has a true calling and the makings of a good religious."

The first questioning of her vocation may occur when a girl realizes she must sacrifice all that is free and familiar to become a nun, but the real soul-searching and self-discipline begin when she enters the convent to start her six months of postulancy. As a postulant she learns the "ABC's" of her religion and is slowly introduced to the disciplines of religious life and to the meaning of the vows she proposes to take in profession. These provisionary six months are followed by the novitiate, a two-year period of intense study, self-scrutiny, discipline, work, and prayer. The first two and a half years of convent life are spiritually and emotionally so exacting that a true vocation is strengthened at the same time that the illusory vocation is eliminated. During this training, a girl's adolescent conviction that she has been called to serve God will be stripped of its protective dreams and plumbed to its depths. If her vocation is real, the dialogue of self and soul, so easily begun in adolescence, deepens and develops, continuing long after the first profession of vows. Over the years it will change her utterly and infuse her with a greater strength and deeper joy than she believed possible. For hers will be that rare certainty few humans enjoy: the conviction that she is "in God's hands, bending her will to His will."

No one vocation is like another; each would-be nun finds her way to this profound certainty differently. Most feel they are called early in life and enter in adolescence; others find after years in the world that they must seek a separate pathway. One Sister of the Missionary Society of Mary, an active group known as the Marist Missionary Sisters, had been a doctor in Paris and a member of the French Underground during World War II. "I had seen much of God's world, much of its sin and suffering," she said. "I found finally I must put myself in His hands and serve as best I could." Few who enter have her maturity or experience, and therefore few can so simply and humbly place themselves "in God's hands." Most must follow a shadowed path that leads inward toward the truth in their own hearts. On the way, if they are fortunate, they will gain maturity, and as each grows in self-discovery each finds her own special "revelation."

Because every vocation is unique, the early signs of a religious calling differ. "You'd like God to call you – to hear His voice – but you don't," said a newly professed member of the society. "You keep expecting that kind of certainty and it doesn't come. Then you start to build it from within yourself and you learn not to expect special miracles. It was because I was foolish enough to want my own special miracle that I had such a struggle." Another newly professed Marist sister admitted, "I didn't really want a vocation and I prayed, 'Please, please God, don't want me.' I thought I wanted to be a journalist and until my senior year in college I fought with myself. I never heard God calling but, as unbelievable as it sounds, I did finally have an intuitive feeling that I'd never be happy unless I became a religious and gave my all to God."

Some come to the convent plagued with doubt, convinced that their ties with the world cannot be broken, to find as time passes a growing serenity. A recently professed Marist sister had been sure she could not abandon "boys and water skiing," and in the weeks just before entering the convent thought she did not have a real vocation. "My father told me not to brainwash myself, not to hide my doubts, but to go ahead and try it. I actually entered not knowing I wanted to stay, and at first it was simply stubborn pride that kept me here."

Others who come believing that they have been truly called discover they have followed dreams of their own making. Cathy Clark, a nineteen-year-old who applied to and was accepted by the Marist Missionary Sisters, was a typical candidate. She had begun thinking about becoming a nun when she was in grammar school. "It's the kind of thing a little girl dreams about," she said. "I had sisters for teachers and it seemed they were so perfect that I wanted to be like them." Cathy's parents were devout and a beloved aunt was a nun; to Cathy her rustling robes whispered of saintliness. "I thought the only way to serve God was this way."

For a sixth-grade assignment Cathy wrote to the sisters and began to learn about them. The Society of Mary, an order of missionary priests, was founded in France in 1816, and the branch of missionary sisters was established thirty years later. The Marist sisters had a proud history as the first women missionaries to the South Pacific. Cathy kept writing to them, and as the correspondence flourished her desire to become a missionary sister grew. "It wasn't really that I saw myself living a great adventure in some exotic land. I knew there was a lot about mission life that was dull, but I thought I ought to give God just a little more by doing something more difficult... I didn't decide anything until my senior year in high school and then the struggle really started." This was just before she entered a convent. "All of a sudden, even though I've always known what a responsibility it was to join, I began to realize what I had to give up. I couldn't do it emotionally. I couldn't do it by myself. It was only the grace of God that would carry me through."

Cathy's last weeks at home seemed to fly past. She found that she had long taken for granted things which now assumed a bright preciousness. In her diary she wrote: "Everything stands out in my mind with such clarity—the freedom to go to the movies, to parties, to see people I love, to date. Even the idea of relaxing in the bath reading a magazine suddenly seems to be something I don't want to give up. I want to turn back, to run the other way—but I love God and know this is what He wants of me."

Had the Marists' Mistress of Postulants known what Cathy was going through she might have counseled her not to enter the convent, or at least to wait a year. But Cathy did not confide in her. "I'm trying to cram a lifetime into a few weeks," she said. "If I think about it any length of time I get so upset." She wrote, "Think how pleased God must be with all the love that these sacrifices prove is His," but this diary entry was surrounded by others, less promising: "I'm miserable." "Another bad day..." "I'm trying to numb myself...."

Her moods swung violently from religious euphoria to adolescent depression. At a football game with her parents she exhibited the noisy enthusiasm of any girl watching strong young men at play—but on the way home in the car that evening she dropped into cold fear, recorded in her diary: "Coming home I wished we might all turn to stone—that time would stop where it was, all of us together."

Superficially Cathy was an impressive candidate for religious life. When she talked to the priest who was her adviser she said all the right things—the things she knew she should say. She was not pretending to have a vocation and sincerely believed that her doubts, depressions, and confusions were of no consequence. When the Marist Mistress of Postulants saw her in a series of pre-entry interviews, she was docile, sweet, and apparently completely happy with her decision to give her life in God's service.

"After all," she was fond of saying, "I'm getting the Son of God Himself."

Even to her parents Cathy was convincing, though her mother had moments of painful misgiving as she watched Cathy running to life—laughing at a twist party, crying over a boy friend's poems, clinging to her father in a moment of fear. Margaret Clark debated whether she ought not counsel Cathy to wait a year before entering, but her selfless zeal prevented her from doing this. She was afraid her own sadness at the separation from her daughter might be influencing her. "I just pretend it's not happening," she said miserably, "and that way I can get through the days. If I let myself think about it, I think I'd grab hold of Cathy so tight that she would never get away."

Cathy realized her mother's unhappiness. "As hard as it is on me," she said, "I can see it's harder for them. They are so generous—they are trying to make it easy for me and it makes me love them more and want to give them more by living my life for God. It's as simple as love, having a vocation. I can leave my parents because they have taught me to love God more than anything else—and I feel He is asking me to do just a little bit more for him than I could if I did not become a nun."

Cathy marched stanchly through the last days. She bought her heavy, practical nun's shoes, remarking, "They don't even look like there's a foot in them." She gave her jewelry to her mother, and her bright clothes to a teen-age cousin. She drank wine at her farewell supper and then, with her little sister Ann looking on, packed her bags for the convent. "Why don't you not be a sister?" pleaded five-year-old Ann—the only member of the family able to watch Cathy pack for departure. "Be a mommy instead and stay home where we can see you." Cathy wept, holding Ann in her arms.

The Clarks drove her to the convent the next day, arriving well before the afternoon deadline of four o'clock. Cathy was calm. Other girls in her class of postulants were there, already dressed in their black habits, strolling the convent grounds with their parents. Some mothers and fathers were weeping; some stood in hushed groups, faces frozen, attempting to talk.

The Clarks held themselves in rigid control while Cathy went upstairs with the Mistress of Postulants to dress in her dark habit and tuck her blond hair under a small black veil. When a novice handed her a mirror her face glowed with pleasure and wonder. There it was at last —all her dreams and struggles culminating in the image of herself as a sister and servant of God. "Oh, my gosh, is it really me?" Then, smiling with wonder, she went downstairs to where her parents waited, suspended in grief, aware of nothing but the clock's steady tick and the passage of time. As Cathy entered, Margaret Clark looked up. For a fleeting moment her face reflected the joy she saw in Cathy's smile—then it clouded. In a rush, the mother had seen how short life is—how quickly a child moves away to her own destiny. "Oh, my Cathy. You look so beautiful, dear! Cathy, Cathy, Cathy, Cathy..." she cried. Cathy leaned on her mother's shoulder, her own face streaming with tears. "Please don't cry," her mother murmured. "Please don't cry, my baby, my baby."

At four-thirty the postulants and their parents climbed the stairs to the convent chapel and Benediction. The girls knelt with the sisters in the front of the chapel and their parents knelt behind them. Then the moment of separation came. "When I walked up those stairs," Cathy recalls, "I thought my heart would break. I almost dreaded God. If God is love, why did it hurt so much?" Cathy heard Ann's voice calling from the back of the chapel: "Cathy, my Cathy. Mommy, why has Cathy left us?"

The next morning Cathy and the other postulants rose at five-forty-five. They had observed what the nuns call the "grand silence": following prayers the night before they were not to speak until after breakfast. Silently they fumbled into unfamiliar habits, helped by the novices. "I wasn't lonesome, just new," recalls Cathy. 'It was even funny. Some sisters even got their habits on backwards."

For the first few days, she was hopeful. "I thought everything would be all right. They say if you can last a week you've got a chance." But soon she began to feel trapped. "There were cans and can'ts for every minute of the day. There was a time to wash, a way to make your bed. Each day it added up; it kept coming and coming."

Mother General Mary Cyr described the postulancy as a period of testing and examination. "We study the girls and learn about them and they study us. I want them to know early what they are giving up in the world. I stress obedience as the hardest of the three vows—for you must give up your will for the will of God as manifested to you by those appointed to lead you to God. It's not the big things they find hard. It's the giving up of self in the details of every-day life."

Cathy began to discover that this kind of obedience demanded more than she was able to give. Her sacrifice was to be of herself. To attain the larger and gentler life of the spirit a sister must empty herself of private wishes, of her desire for home and family, of heroic dreams of serving God, and become a selfless vessel, entirely acquiescent to God's will and grace. To open her heart to Him, she attempts to erase all private affections and submit her whole being to the sisterhood and the Rule which guides it. By this strict compliance with the discipline which governs every moment of convent life, she is led slowly to a deepening spiritual awareness that finds God's will manifest in all things. Only if she is able to commit her innermost being to this life of prayer and discipline will a postulant go onward to profession.

Cathy Clark wanted to give herself as she was to God—but she could not bring herself to make the total commitment demanded and begin life over from within. The essential meta-morphosis from private emotion to selfless love was beyond her. She was too strongly attached to home, to parents and friends, to be able to enlarge and generalize her emotions to include all her sisters and those she would serve in the world as equal sharers of her heart. "I thought I could be the same me, loving and serving God," she said, "but I found this wasn't so. I thought detachment meant leaving my family and friends physically but taking them with me in my love for them. That's not what it is; a nun has to learn to love in a different way." Because she could not cut the ties that bound her to the world, Cathy lost her vocation. Instead of finding a growing peace and pleasure in her commitment, she felt stifled, cut off from life, and unnatural.

During this early period the superiors observe each girl's conflicts. A "Mother" is always in charge of education of the young postulants and novices. A "Sister" does not have the responsibility of guiding the young ones spiritually after they are received as novices. If they feel she strains too much, that her emotions are extreme or shaky, or that she will not be able to bear the harsh demands of mission life, they are quick to guide her and will advise her to leave if necessary. Cathy was one advised to leave. "I was so lonely and unhappy," she recalls, "I couldn't sleep and sometimes I couldn't really pray." After a month in the convent she was called by the Mistress of Postulants. Cathy remembers the day. "She took me to a different section of the convent where she said, 'Put on your clothes, child, your folks will be here soon.' I didn't even say good-by—that made me sad, but now I'm the happiest reject on the face of the earth. I am content just to serve God in the world."

As a Marist reject, Cathy was far more typical than those whom "God chooses." In the last fifteen years the Marists have corresponded with over nine hundred girls. A third have been refused, a third joined other communities, and three hundred joined the Marists. "But that does not mean all have persevered," said the Mother General. "More than a hundred have left. About thirty left on their own, and the others were dismissed for reasons of health or character. All who have entered and left know themselves better and are the better for having come here. Those who stay grow stronger. God chooses whom He wills, and once He's made His choice He does not change His mind."

PAGES

17   *In her last days at home, Marist candidate Cathy Clark, overwhelmed by fears of entering the convent, seeks consolation in her father's arms.*

18-19   *Nineteen-year-old Cathy enjoys her last fling of freedom: at a football game, window shopping, and dancing at a farewell twist party.*

20-21   *Family supper and her father's toast mark the final day at home. Cathy's mother looks on sadly, unable to join in the toast.*

22-23   *Dressed in the habit and veil of a Marist Missionary postulant, Cathy shouts for joy at her achievement. "Gosh, is it really me?"*

24   *The first sight of Cathy in her habit brings elation, then tears, to her mother.*

25   *Mrs. Clark comforts weeping Cathy: "You look so beautiful, dear."*

26-27   *As Cathy clings to her, her mother whispers gently, "Please don't cry, my baby, my baby."*

28-29   *Dreading the final farewell, Cathy holds on to her father (top left) and tries to comfort her small sister (top center), who did not want her to become a nun. In the last minutes before saying good-by, Cathy reaches for her father's hand (bottom left) and then wipes away his tears (right).*

30-31   *(Top:) Separated from her family, Cathy weeps at Benediction. "When I walked up the stairs," she said later, "I thought my heart would break. If God is love, why did it hurt so much?" (Bottom:) To distract postulants from their unhappiness, the Marists give them small chores such as sewing. The rule of silence is not imposed for several days.*

32   *During the first week, the postulants enjoy extra recreation. Cathy and Sandra Jewel, her best friend, roller-skate with novices at the convent.*

21

CHAPTER

II

Cathy Clark returned to the busy world she wanted; she found a job as a technician in a blood bank and in time fell in love. Marriage, children, a home of her own await her in the future. A wholly different life and love awaited those she had left behind at the convent, to be attained only by a long journey of the spirit.

Recalling that journey, novice Sister Mary Shawn, who had entered the convent with Cathy, was struck with awe. "It seems a long time from the postulancy until now," she said. "You see such vast change in yourself. Nothing else except God's grace very much at work in you could have made such differences. When you see yourself as you were then and as you are now, you know you are not responsible. It gives you a sense of tranquillity and security which sometimes seems more than is right for one so young—especially when I think of the problems faced by girls my age in the world. But *you* haven't attained this security. It's God who has led you and you have simply been going along under his protection. When you realize this, even when the going is slow and hard and you are frightened, you believe that everything will be all right. You no longer think, as I did at first, that it's only when you feel Him and have great joy in Him that you are really close to Him. Now you know that to really draw close to Him you must be drawn by Him when you are most alone. This is His way of uniting you to Him. As a novice, you just taste this; in the missions, professed, you *know* it. Yet even now you feel Him at work in you. You no longer struggle with self so much; you become fascinated with others, part of your sisters. A real charity grows and you enter into the sister-hood as into a family— and that bond absorbs all your thought. Through the love of others, you begin to open your heart. There are no barriers—you have begun to clear the way to Him."

Months had passed into years since Cathy's brief time in the convent. Sandra Jewel had become Sister Mary Shawn. A new class of postulants had entered the convent, some to suffer and discover, as Cathy had, that they were not among those God had chosen for this life, others to know the wonder and joy of following their own special pathways to God. It was winter once again, and the first snowfall brought a desolate splendor to the December landscape. In the predawn darkness of the convent the sisters gathered in their chapel to chant Lauds, the first prayer of the day. Through the silence of the night their voices rose on a single note: "O God, come to my assistance... O Lord, make haste to help me..." As they chanted, the convent bells tolled dawn's break to the sleeping world beyond their walls, and the sun brightened the stained-glass windows of the chapel to reveal the Lamb of God, splendid in the golden rays. Within the chapel, night's gloom still prevailed, and the veiled sisters seemed momentarily priestesses of some ancient rite suspended in eternal devotion. Their voices rose with a psalm of praise: "He sends forth His command to the earth.... He spreads snow like wool, frost He strews like ashes. He scatters hail like crumbs; before His cold the waters freeze. He sends His word and melts them; He lets His breeze blow and the waters run. He has proclaimed His word to Jacob, His statutes and His ordinances to Israel ... Glorify the Lord, O Jerusalem."

The season of Advent had begun. For the postulants and novices struggling to prepare themselves for profession, the coming of Christmas seemed a light at the dark midpoint of their journey through the year. The great feast promised that their days and years of discipline would be blessed as surely as spring would come to refresh the earth after the silent sleep of winter. Christ's birth pointed the way to Calvary and the redemption of all mankind.

The new postulants were now halfway through their six months of preparation. Those who remained realized they had only just begun to understand the demands of vocation. During Advent they heard again the call, "Prepare ye the way of the Lord. Make straight in the wilderness the paths of our God," that had brought them to the convent. Now the full meaning of this task was becoming clear. "If anyone will come after me, let him deny himself and take up his cross and follow me...." Many young sisters faltered and looked longingly back to other Christmases bright with the lights on a sparkling tree, warm with the laughter of families now far away. At this season, home called with an undeniable poignance. A postulant, watching the snow etch the dark boughs of a tall spruce, spoke for all when she murmured sadly, "It's like the woods at home where we cut our tree each Christmas."

"We know," said the Mistress of Postulants, Sister Mary Luke, "that this is one of the hardest times of the postulancy, and we are patient with them. But it is also a time to take stock. After three months we believe they should have absorbed some of the meaning of the vows they hope to take and some of the reasons for the Rule. Until now the main difference between the novice and the postulant has been that we have not been as strict with the postulant. We have not scolded when she failed to do as instructed, have let her be herself and talk much of the time. But now we feel the time has come to begin to live by the Rule—for it is designed to lead her to God."

With stern wisdom she tells them that their own homesickness is a sign of failure. "You cannot give yourself halfway to God," she says firmly in one of their daily conferences to review progress, "holding back from Him the love you have given your family. You have been called to an absolute sacrifice by His love for you. You must remember that when two people love each other the slightest inconsideration of one wounds the other. The decision to give yourself to God must be unreserved, for it will wound Christ's heart, which is an abyss of love. Give Him your heartache. Turn your thoughts only to Him and you can gain for your families a supernatural grace that could never otherwise be theirs. Let your sisters be your family," she continues, in gentle admonishment. "Did not Christ tell us: 'Everyone who has left house or brothers or sisters or father or mother or children or lands for my name's sake shall receive in the present time a hundredfold as much houses and brothers and sisters and children and lands—along with persecutions—and in the age to come life everlasting'? You are entering a new family — one that includes your own but one which is much greater."

To coerce these gentle changes in a postulant's heart, much more than Scripture and command are used. The whole routine of convent life, the long hours of each day, the cycle of prayer that divides the day into the Little Hours and the week into a stately procession tracing the Word of God from Old Testament to New, and even the prescribed program of work and recreation, are part of a carefully considered psychological plan moving step by step along the path of spiritual development. In the all-embracing ritual of the day, the postulants begin to feel that they live outside the world's time. Everything they do is woven into the web of reverence which spins days into weeks and weeks into months. The bell that calls them now to work and now to prayer becomes eventually "His voice calling you."

But for a while the postulants rebel. "They are afraid of losing their identity," explained Sister Mary Luke understandingly. "They wonder, in dressing alike, acting at the same time in the same way, if they are not simply disappearing as individuals. They hate the restrictions of a full schedule that permits no time to rest or go off by yourself. They don't like to have to ask permission of superiors to make the slightest change in their routine. Naturally, they show it." Though outwardly the girls conform to the Rule, their rebellion appears in a dozen small and subtle ways. It is there in their irrepressible gaiety, in their postures and gestures, even in the small freedoms of dress allowed to them. A postulant wearing bright-red sneakers, emerging feet first from inside a great oven she had been cleaning, is pulled out by one of her young sisters. The cooperative task of dish-washing finds three silent postulants far wetter than they need to be. By contrast with the novices, who seem to float about their kitchen work a few inches off the floor suspended on a nimbus of silence, the postulants cavort like kittens, sprinkling the conversation necessary to their duties with laughter and teasing. "The postulants are crows," said the Mother General laughingly, "they say no, no, no. The novices are doves, they murmur yes, yes, yes."

Perhaps most difficult for the postulant are the long periods of silence demanded by the Rule. In the morning from five-twenty-five until ten-thirty they are expected to restrict themselves to talk which contributes to their study, their work, or their prayer. The first free period of ten minutes, given the blessing of the Mistress of Postulants by the words "Deo gratias," is greeted with the kind of noisy enthusiasm characteristic of small children escaping school. "Silence is hard for them at first," said Sister Mary Luke. "They want to distract themselves from the real meaning of religious life with worldly concerns. But in time they learn that the purpose of our silence is to be recollected in full concentration upon God throughout the day. For, though He is in all things, we cannot see Him unless we are empty of all but thought for Him. The outer silence demanded by the Rule is only to obtain an inner silence that we may know Him."

As the sense of serenity and inner silence grows, the tranquil rhythms of convent life and its routine of work, prayer, and study become more and more satisfying to the postulants. A stately significance is lent to their young lives; the hours of the day move by like a tapestry, the meaning of each of the day's occupations inextricably bound into their central devotion to Christ. The Little Hour of Terce, preceding housework, reminds them that their true home is the "House of God." "How lovely is your dwelling place, O Lord of Hosts...." The simple tasks that keep the convent shining, the altar flowers fresh, and the kitchen fragrant with cooking contribute to a comforting sense of belonging to a new "home" and "family" in which work is blessed as "prayer of the hands."

When the bell calls them from their chores to chapel for the chanting of Sext, their minds are already gently with God. A single note rises in the silence with the same haunting refrain that began the day in darkness: "O God, come to my assistance; O Lord, make haste to help me...." Like a strophe in the chorus of hours, the psalm tells them that day is half done, the cycle of prayer turned halfway in its eternal circle through darkness and light. It is time for the second meditation demanded by the Rule, the Particular Examine.

In the brightness of midday they turn their eyes inward to search for the small ways they have failed God. During their training they have been taught to analyze themselves according to three main categories called by the superiors the "threefold concupiscences." "These are the concupiscence of life, of the eyes, and of the flesh," Novice Mistress Mother Mary Regis explained. "Because of them we fall roughly into three categories. The cholerics are those who do not recognize God's will in their lives and their complete dependence upon Him. Their greatest task is obedience, which helps us to weaken pride by accepting the will of our superiors. Those of a possessive nature—the second type—bog down in things and creatures instead of using creation to lead them upward to God. The appetites of the eyes dominate them. Poverty helps to weaken this inordinate desire and to detach us from anything which could prevent us from giving ourselves wholly to God. The third category consists of those who have an inordinate attachment to themselves, to their own comfort, or to others; they suffer the weakness of the flesh, which may form a block between themselves and God. Our object is never to love any *one* more than God. Our vow of chastity is meant to counteract the tendencies of the flesh. It is a very positive thing, for it allows you to give yourself completely to God and frees you from this inordinate pull."

What begins as a difficult discipline of self-analysis and control slowly becomes a joy of inner discovery that brings a sense of enrichment to the postulant. Her life has become infused with meaning—her sense of purpose in her vocation is strengthening and she begins to look forward to the novitiate and profession rather than backward to the world she has sacrificed.

Often now she is rewarded by an overwhelming happiness and sense of closeness to God. Familiar prayers such as the "Hail Mary" have taken on glowing meaning for her, for she feels that as she lives in imitation of the Blessed Mother she too may know the profound joy of becoming "full of grace," "blessed amongst women," and live with the Lord always. No longer hesitant and afraid, she becomes surer that she is among those whom God has chosen.

"There is great joy in this life," said Mother Mary Regis, "for as you empty yourself, there is more room for Him. We emphasize the positive today and help them to realize God's tremendous love for them as well as helping them to understand what He expects of them. For each one is loved by Him as an individual. This is one of the basic things. To know God's love for you provides the motivation to serve Him. They may know this love by studying how much they have received from Him. All that they have is a gift of God—and so they must share it with each other and offer it for His greater glory."

In time convent life becomes an expression of love for the young sisters. As they give openly to each other, they give to God. They have become less and less concerned with themselves, more and more concerned with the community and the work of the sisterhood. An expression of the growth of this familial bond within the convent and the joy the girls feel in pursuing religious life explodes during a pre-Christmas pageant offered to their Superior, Mother Mary Ambrose, as a gift on her feast day. A few days before the celebration, "Deo gratias" frees all for long evenings of recreation and rehearsal, and the postulants and novices make the most of their opportunity to laugh, sing, and dance together in the preparation of skits.

On the evening of the pageant the convent hall is darkened and all the sisters—professed, postulants, and novices—gather to offer their "Mother" the gifts of talent God has given them. A spotlight picks out four novices dancing, their white veils sweeping in smooth strokes through the darkness. One emerges as a soloist, pirouetting gracefully on toe point. Pink beribboned ballet slippers flash beneath her long black habit, and in her hands a flow of sparkling tinsel catches the light as she weaves a silent song that is all youth. The shroud of her habit and the sweep of her veil become a flow of ultimate grace above the swift pink slippers.

This is a varied pageant. Four postulants dressed in grass skirts perform a Fiji dance. From the missions in Peru the professed sisters bring a *piñata*—a large, brightly wrapped bundle that hangs overhead and swirls a shower of candy over the laughing audience. From a face impassive by day a rich voice, in fluent Spanish, intones a lovely carol without a trace of shyness, as a gift to Mother, to the Marist family, and to the Christ Child, whose birth it tells.

In a few days, Christmas, God's great gift to man, comes and goes. The days lengthen toward spring and the postulants find that they no longer struggle with the hold of the past. They have begun to move toward an inner silence and selflessness. But now a new and frightening experience comes to many. They no longer "feel" God's presence. In the silence and routine they seem to have lost Him and the joy they first felt in following a vocation. Each is alone and uncertain. "Some leave the convent when this happens," said Sister Mary Luke.

"Some become rigid and begin to lean on the Rule for the Rule's sake. They search for strictness and use the objects of religious life as a substitute for the living spirit. Some run away to books or to work; they want distractions from their loneliness. Some fall back entirely upon themselves and begin to assert their own strength instead of relying on God. Depending upon how long this first period of aridity lasts, it can be the first real crisis of religious life. The postulant thinks God has abandoned her until she makes the great discovery that this is the substance of Scripture: God has always led his chosen people from fear to love. She looks around her and sees in the thoughtfulness of her sisters that He is still present. A subtle change begins. Until now, her mistake has been the alliance of the idea of pleasure with love. When it becomes sacrifice—when in her pain she is still bent on accepting His will and pleasing Him; when she realizes, in fact, that religion is not emotion, she has taken a great stride. For God wants us to know Him without seeing, without feeling, without reasoning Him. We must leap into faith through Christ's life. It is only by committing ourselves in this total darkness—by loving the Giver and not His gifts, that we can attain the aim of our life. The function of the six months of postulancy is to arm beforehand for this darkness and to plant the seed of grace that will grow in the dark and bring them to God."

In the next two years that seed of grace will be nurtured by a study of religious history and Scripture, by a careful indoctrination into the great cycle of the prayer year, by meticulous examination of each girl's strengths and weaknesses conducted by her superiors. Spiritual darkness will come to be accepted as a test of faith. "This is a purification process," said the Novice Mistress, "and by repeated experience of aridity they grow stronger. As one goes along the periods are prolonged, and one must depend more and more upon simple faith. And so, gradually, real faith grows to replace emotionalism; they realize that just as psychological maturity is gained by meeting crises and enduring anxieties, so spiritual maturity is gained. We take a long time in preparing them for acceptance of this darkness that comes and goes —and they learn finally to accept it as part of His plan for them. They realize they need never doubt *His* strength, only their own—that His love is everlasting and beyond question. So they become secure in it and depend only on Him. Once they have tested the love of Christ, they are led back to Him again and again by the joy of that experience—even through the profoundest darkness. Nothing else is satisfying."

The first experience of aridity is a terrifying thing, through which no postulant or novice passes without pain. Yet, as if to emphasize her need to face her isolation before God, the postulant must enter a retreat of eight days' silence before reception as a novice. There is nothing in her sixteen-hour day to distract her from that "inner silence" where she is alone with God. There are no books, no recreation, no mail. Even housework is cut to a minimum, and small fasts are imposed. "Silence and separation are our spiritual food and drink," she is counseled. In deepest concentration, the postulant meditates upon her weaknesses and tries to erase all distractions and emotions that keep her from recollection and total dedication to God. She broods upon Christ's life and the agonies that led to Calvary as she says the stations of the cross in the last deep snows of winter. Though the postulants are physically together during retreat, each feels herself utterly alone before Him, utterly unworthy. Rebellion has been left behind now, and she prays only that God may find all acceptable and that all may hereafter live entirely "in His hands." Following a general confession which reviews her whole life, she is at last ready to move forward in religion and receive the veil of a novice.

The Reception Ceremony is held with only the Marist sisters as witnesses. In silent excitement, the postulants cover their short hair with a white cap, over which the lovely white veil is folded. Then all kneel at the altar and each receives a small white card bearing her new name in religion. Henceforth she will be known only by this name. Her identity has changed from that of her own family to that of the Marist family—a change symbolic of all that has happened within her heart. The new name is compounded from that of the Blessed Mother, to whom the Marists are dedicated, and a saint's name bearing some connection to the girl or to her family. It is chosen by her superiors, though it may be one from a list of three submitted before reception by each postulant. Whatever the name, each girl seems thrilled by the change, for it means she is truly one with her sisters and accepted by God to continue the spiritual journey toward Him.

"It had been such a long hard struggle," recalled Sister Mary Jan, the former Theresa Pasterczyk, just after her reception, "but when the day came for my pretty white veil and my new name, I knew I didn't want to be Theresa any more, but Sister Mary Jan. I had left the past behind me and I knew at last that God wanted me, even homely me." Sister Mary Jan was named for her mother's favorite saint, the little-known Jan who had been patron of her native village of Dukla in Poland. "With reception," said the Mistress of Postulants, "they have learned we are all one in God. Through their sisters they see the beauty of the Holy Spirit at work, the eternal circle of the Trinity which binds Father, Son, and Holy Spirit in love. It is within this circle that they move forward toward profession. It is a time of great joy."

Reverence bursts with this joy when reception is over. The new novices, breaking their eight-day silence, erupt with excitement as they use each other's new names and admire their flowing white veils. A whole afternoon of freedom and, "Deo gratias," of talk is theirs. They dash through the last snows of winter on a hike and mischievously pelt one another with snowballs as they let off some of the pent-up exuberance of youth. For the first time in weeks they chatter during their afternoon snack of peanut-butter-and-jelly sandwiches—and laugh as only the young can, with a joyous sense of accomplishment. They are ready now to move onward to the serious business of the novitiate—the two years of study which are considered the foundation of the religious life. Though profession is still two years away, they have already learned much. "They have grown simpler and more childlike. They are closer to God now—ready to be taught by Him."

PAGES

41   During the daily recitation of the rosary, a postulant broods on the crucifixion in the snow-bound garden of the convent.

42-43   The life of silence and obedience leads to an increasing awareness of God. (Bottom right:) The bell, which signals the hours of prayer, work, and study, becomes "His voice calling."

44-45   Each moment of a postulant's day is rigidly planned. Prayers of the Little Hours, daily chores regarded as "prayers of the hands," and even instruction periods are offered to God. Postulants and novices, although they are allowed to sit, eschew comfort and (bottom left) stand at the midmorning snack.

46-47   Six months of postulancy end with the Reception Ceremony, when candidates are "accepted by God." In moments of silent joy before reception, the novice's white veil replaces the black net of postulancy. (Bottom right:) In a private Reception Ceremony, the novices kneel to kiss the medal they will receive and are given cards bearing their new names in religion.

48-49   As she receives her new name, Theresa Pasterczyk glows with happiness. "I knew I didn't want to be Theresa any more," she said, "but Sister Mary Jan...."

50-51   After the Reception Ceremony, new novices are led on a two-mile hike by Marist Superior Mother Mary Ambrose, a former diving champion and a mission veteran.

52-53   Breaking the silence of an eight-day retreat which preceded the Reception Ceremony, the new novices cavort in the snow during the recreation.

54-55   The midafternoon treat of sandwiches and freedom to talk are part of new novice's reward at the end of six months' postulancy.

56   Marists do most of their own work at the convent. Even novices who are engrossed in intense spiritual training must do heavy chores such as clearing snow.

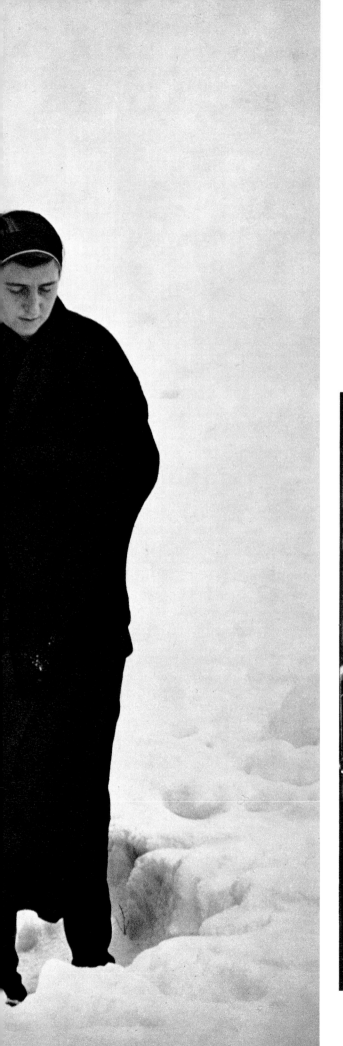

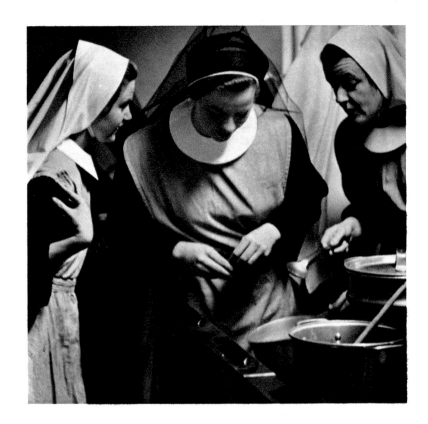

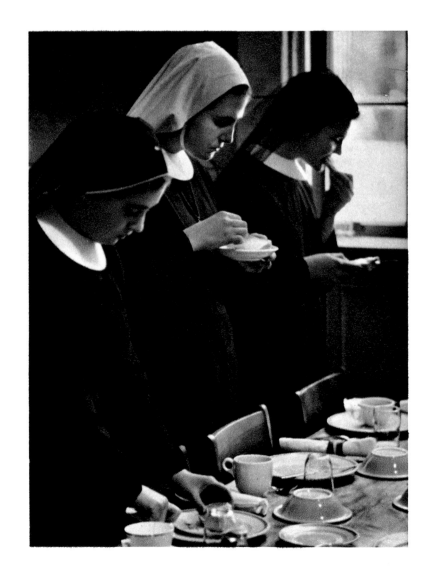

CHAPTER
III

With the Reception Ceremony a phase of religious life begins for which the novice's white veil and new name are suitable symbols. The two-year novitiate tests each girl so deeply that at its end she feels she has been spiritually reborn. Under the guidance of her Mistress, the novice enters a world of spirit within herself, recapturing the innocent awe of childhood. She develops a kind of "second sight" which infuses all reality with the shimmering presence of God and causes silence to thunder with His voice. The novice is enthralled; her romance of the spirit excludes all other interests, heightens every action and prayer until they assume an importance not unlike the incandescence with which young love imbues its private world. The familiar "Our Father" is no longer a formal prayer but a personal statement. It expresses what is in her heart: "Hallowed be Thy name—Thy kingdom come, Thy will be done on earth as it is in heaven." As she moves through her day the Gloria rings in her mind: "Glory be to the Father, and to the Son and to the Holy Spirit—as it was in the beginning, is now, and ever shall be, world without end."

These are the "foundation years of spiritual development." During them, the novice makes a commitment to God to "renew from within by letting Christ live in her heart." She believes that everything which keeps her from this goal, everything which calls her back to her old self, must be transformed and redirected. When she feels utterly open to His command her happiness is intense, but when she finds emptiness within, and is drawn back to private emotions and memories, she feels a failure and is deeply lonely.

"We know that it is not natural for a young girl to separate herself so entirely from the world," said Mother Mary Ambrose, "but she seeks a life above nature—a supernatural life. Her aim is perfection and ultimately union with God. The higher the goal, the stricter the pathway to reach it." For the novice, the only possible way to achieve "union with God in heaven" is to follow Christ's life and offer during her lifetime a "death of self" as a fitting sacrifice for the gift of "life everlasting." To achieve this, she willingly accepts an increasing austerity in her life and slowly subjects her inmost being to the Rule of the Missionary Sisters of the Society of Mary, which she believes has been "designed to lead her to God."

In time she will be brought back from the recesses of her spiritual journey to join her sisters actively working in the world as missionaries. But for the two and a half years of the novitiate she follows a pathway toward eternity, the pathway of prayer and adoration of God pursued for life by those other religious called to contemplative life. For this brief time she shares with them a call to live outside of time, beyond temporal concerns, beyond human need, in pure devotion to the vision of God and thoughts of his awesome and eternal power. The more she realizes this vision, and the more she places her reliance on His plan and His will, the more aware she becomes of the smallness of her own life and of the work she may do in her brief time on earth. She will be guided by this awareness in years to come. When her mission work seems to be of immediate and overwhelming importance, when frustration and grief in her confrontation of human suffering threaten her faith, she will be able to turn inward to recapture a sense of the smallness of each life and the profundity of God's plan for all existence.

Outwardly, little of the great spiritual adventure of the novitiate shows; the novice's life differs only slightly from the basic routine followed in the postulate. The bell still rings the sixteen-hour day to its ordered schedule. The food is the same. Novices sleep in the same kind of simple rooms on narrow cots; besides a cross upon the wall, a small chest and a chair for each sister are the only other furnishings. All possessions, including their two habits and three veils, are considered as belonging to the community, and the only personal things a novice has are her pajamas, underwear, a watch, a fountain pen, and a family photograph.

What changes is the unseen world. During the canonical year the novices' links with the outside are severely curtailed. The first year is a concentrated one. It is only through isolation that they may gain enough purity of spirit to establish a contact with Christ and begin to know Him. Mother Mary Regis explained, "Once you know His love, His plan for you, His gift to you even of trials, you will never be overwhelmed. You have the strength of Christ to bring you through any ordeal. It is something you can't get from reading about it. You must be withdrawn long enough to develop convictions inside yourself. You must follow Christ's example and retire from the world completely until your thoughts are formed."

For this reason, the novice may receive mail only once a week and may write home only once a month. Letters to and from her may be read by her superiors so that they can be aware of anything that might disrupt her spiritual progress. Family visits are limited to four a year and last only a few hours.

To enhance the isolation in which spiritual life flourishes, the period of silence—except when duties require speech—is extended to all but an hour and a half of the day. In addition, the novice is bound to take "custody over her eyes, the window of the soul" and through self-discipline to cut off all in her range of vision that might distract her from inner concentration. Symbolically, she is to blind herself to all that invites her interest or desires, except God. Her aim is "only the divine," and in the vows she intends to take in profession she expects to consecrate "her body and soul completely to Him" by undertaking to "watch over her senses, especially the eyes, to watch over her memory, her imagination, her reading, and other forms of relaxation, to watch over her heart, refusing to allow any affection that is purely natural or merely a matter of feeling." During the novitiate she begins to exercise the controls that will bring her to the point where she can promise such devotion.

The program of formal study is also increased in quantity and quality during the novitiate. Seventeen hours a week are spent in class and prescribed studies pursuing such heavy subjects as ascetical theology, moral theology, liturgy, Scripture, and religious history. Essentially the canonical year is devoted to a study of the Old Testament, and the new novices are taught to see parallels between God's treatment of His chosen people and the spiritual journey upon which they have embarked. The teachers point out that the Jews kept faith and persevered through great trial in God's service because they recognized and feared His total power over all creation. As the Jews were led by the belief that one day God would send a Messiah with a message of love and redemption, so the novices must be led through their own times of fear and loneliness until they pass beyond them to know, on faith, God's love for them. They come to believe that their dependence upon Him is complete, that they must submit to Him entirely, and that ultimately they will be rewarded by the love of the Son of God which will be theirs in Paradise. To know and understand this love, they will spend the second year in the novitiate studying the life of Christ and the Holy Family at Nazareth so that they may better imitate Him and the spirit of His Blessed Mother.

The relationship between the symbolic meanings of Scripture and the philosophy of their faith is made abundantly clear by the priests and superiors who teach the novices. Under their tutelage, a related vision of human life as part of the awesome tapestry of creation begins to emerge—and in that tapestry each young nun believes a plan for her exists. Spiritual meanings appear to pervade everything the novice sees, does, and says. Her daily prayers of the Office, the lives of the saints chosen as the day's lesson, the readings from Scripture and theology that she hears at meals, the magnificent pattern of the Little Hours through the weeks and months of the year—all begin to reveal inner meanings proving God's profound plan. So ordered seem the ways of the universe, so absolute His knowledge, that the novice no longer finds reason to doubt except through her own fault. At last it seems to each that she has begun to understand, and—understanding—she must comply.

"When she attains this vision, obedience, acceptance, and love are almost automatic," said Mother Mary Regis. "She can get through the darkest moments of emptiness and come out stronger for them. In the courtship of the novitiate, she is led along to ever-increasing love of God. She knows that love best when He seems not to be present—by the degree of yearning she feels for Him. Eventually, she has the wonderful security that comes with knowing she has the best—and so she searches Scripture and prayer the better to understand Him. She is impatient with anything that obstructs her now, impatient of the weakness of her self and her self-love. She wants room in her soul only for Him and she realizes He has planned her life for her purification, her sanctification, her growth with Him."

Nothing else is important to the novice when she reaches this stage of spiritual development except that she make herself worthy of God and eventually profess herself to Him. She lives outside time—except as it is "His time." She offers her six hours of prayer each day as a part of the great chorus of devotion that the earth itself gives to God. She and her sisters around the world, through the cyclic passing hours, in the unfolding magnificence of day and night, offer unending praise to Him. The Church rings the seasons with prayer, and the sisterhood circles the globe with devotion. As she knows in the very center of her being, this unending chorus of praise is only fitting, for all are "in His hands." At day's end, when the silver chime of the bell calls her to Vespers, she joins in the haunting invocation: "O God, come to my assistance, O Lord, make haste to help me." Her voice rises with the others in the psalm:

"O Lord, you have probed me and you know me;
You know when I sit and when I stand;
you understand my thoughts from afar.
My journeys and my rest you scrutinize,
with all my ways you are familiar.
Even before a word is on my tongue,
behold, O Lord, you know the whole of it.
Behind me and before, you hem me in
and rest your hand upon me.
Such knowledge is too wonderful for me;
too lofty for me to attain.
Where can I go from your spirit:
from your presence where can I flee?
If I go up to the heavens, you are there;
If I sink to the nether world, you are present there.
If I take the wings of dawn,
if I settle at the farthest limits of the sea,
Even there your hand shall guide me,
and your right hand hold me fast.
If I say 'Surely the darkness shall hide me,
and night shall be my light—'
For you darkness itself is not dark,
and night shines as the day.
Darkness and light are the same.
Truly you have formed my inmost being;
you knit me in my mother's womb.
I give you thanks that I am fearfully, wonderfully made;

wonderful are your works.

My soul also you knew full well;
nor was my frame unknown to you
when I was made in secret,
when I was fashioned in the depths of the earth.

Your eyes have seen all my actions;
in your book they are all written;
my days were limited before one of them existed.

How weighty are your designs, O God:
how vast the sum of them!

Were I to recount them, they would outnumber the sands;
did I reach the end of them, I should still be with you."

When the interior life gains primacy, there are certain marked changes in the novices. They are rapt in concentration, their silence charged with a dreamlike pensiveness. They slip from place to place, their eyes cast down, their heads bent at a thoughtful angle. Their postures and their gestures become more uniform and graceful, as if the bumps and angles of personal idiosyncrasy had been smoothed away. They seem afloat rather than on foot, and the individual girls appear to have been replaced by a chorus of contemplative spirits. Their hands whisper over the pages when they study, and when they pray they kneel so straight it seems they offer God perfect posture as well as perfect prayer. For hours the only sound in the novitiate is the swish of white veils, the soft, light rhythm of hurrying footsteps, and, periodically, the haunting chant of the Little Hours, piercing the silence. Time passes into the chorus of these Hours; days become years. The canonical novice begins her second year of study, the chaplet year of a novitiate. "The seed of grace has been planted in the darkness—now let His goodness and mercy nurture you. Let us follow Mary and live as the Holy Family did at Nazareth."

To mark the completion of the canonical year, each novice receives a large rosary to hang at her waist. By its beads she will remember the joys and sorrows of Mary as the Blessed Mother followed Christ from the Annunciation until His death.

The chaplet year brings the novice back from the recesses of her spiritual journey into self. The darkness is lit now by love, and she reaches outward to embrace the family of her sisterhood. Recalling her own metamorphosis, a chaplet who had entered the convent in the same class of postulants as Cathy Clark laughed as she said, "I'd never have gotten through the postulancy if I hadn't been so vain. I was going to make it—and that was that. I even thought they needed me in the missions. They don't need *me*—though they are happy to have me join them, happy that I too have been given a gift from God and that all of us are needed for His work. I've learned He is the great one in this affair. It was egotistical to believe I was the center. In fact, I made a point after I entered of looking back on the world as if it were nothing. I was superior to all of that. After a while I realized how good it all was and how much I did enjoy boys and parties and freedom. Slowly I grasped the idea that He had created all of it—that indeed the world was good because it is His. Now I know what I've given up; the dearness of what I've left behind makes me know that what I seek is greater than all else. I only hope He will keep me for profession, for I want to stay with Him and my sisters."

For every novice, profession represents the great beginning of religious life. In taking the three vows of poverty, chastity, and obedience, she believes that she is in effect saying "Yes" to God's plan for her. With these vows, she promises to live at God's side, belonging only to Him and serving Him through love. She looks upon profession as the equivalent of marriage. Her vows mean that she has "forsaken all others," that she will never look back in regret to another life, that she will stifle the lovely songs of memory and the call of her desires for the world. Though, in fact, a Marist novice does not bind herself by perpetual vows until six years after her first profession, she intends that these first vows be absolute, and by their nature they do bind her to the core of her spirit. With them she promises to guard over every distraction from God—to take custody of her eyes, her mind, her imagination, her memory, and her body and place all of herself in God's hands without a single wish but to serve Him. To take such a vow is an awesome step, and at the very last the novice goes through a profound soul-searching to be sure that she is capable of making so great a promise to God.

For Sister Mary Ruth Ann, profession meant the end of a long journey of sacrifice and commitment that had begun when she left home to join the Marists, against her mother's will. In the two and a half years between the terrible parting and the time of her profession she had not seen, spoken to, or heard from her mother. Only her grandparents' letters had kept her informed of her mother's lonely life. In Sister Mary Ruth Ann's memory was forever engraved the picture of the one person she loved most in the world running after a car —sobbing and calling her name. Many times the young novice was torn by a sense of profound selfishness in the following of her vocation. Many times she felt she must turn back— and yet she had not.

On the eve of her profession she struggled still with the specter of grief she had brought to her mother. In her final retreat before profession, she concentrated on the way of the cross, her mind rapt in the sufferings of Christ and of His Mother. As she listened to Mother Mary Ambrose at the rehearsal for the Profession Ceremony, her face turned pensive and her thoughts were far away.

"As long as I could remember," she recalled, "I wanted to be a missionary nun. My grandfather, my grandmother, my mother—everybody tried to persuade me to join an order nearer home or to wait a year, or not to join at all. But this was the only thing I wanted. Oh, I had visions of leading poor souls into heaven with drum and bugle or something. I've learned it isn't like that—but that is *now*. Then, I wanted the missions for all kinds of selfish reasons and I wouldn't be put off.

"When no one in my family would help me, I went to work and saved the train fare to come up here and join the Marists. My grandfather said I could go, but he wasn't going to help me go. I think they all thought I would just join a teaching order close to home. And I remember when the day finally came. My grandfather said he'd drive me to the station. My mother still wouldn't believe I was leaving. I remember the car pulling away from the house and she came running out, calling my name, crying to me to come back. She ran after the car, calling to me. I couldn't look back. I couldn't see, I was crying so hard. I just had to come here.... I just had to come. For two and a half years, I haven't heard from her...."

That night, Sister Mary Ruth Ann was called by the Marist Mother General Mary Cyr for her final interview, the Canonical Examination. By her gentle questions the Mother General finally reviews the candidate's vocation, intentions, and doubts. Her tone is such that each girl is given an opportunity to turn back without a feeling of disgrace or failure. "They must do this of their own free wills," said Mother Mary Cyr, "like children of God. We do not want them forced or persuaded. They must follow from their own hearts. It is to ensure this freedom that we put off perpetual vows until they have had a time in the missions and know truly what this life is like before they bind themselves forever. Yet this first profession is one of love—and as such it is critically important."

Mother Mary Cyr's voice was gentle when Sister Mary Ruth Ann entered. "How are you?" she asked. "How do you feel?" "I am a little more relaxed, Mother. My grandparents are coming. I don't have the confidence that at last my family will be here—but they say they are coming." She looked down, wringing her hands in her lap. "And in the spring, perhaps my mother and my little brother..." She was on the verge of tears, and Mother Mary Cyr waited for a moment before asking the next question. "Did you make a good retreat?" she said quietly.

"I tried, but I don't feel like I'm walking on clouds. I feel I'm capable of improving. I'm so self-centered, so selfish."

Mother Mary Cyr smiled. "That's the spiritual life building."

"But Mother, I feel like I'm just starting out. I feel I haven't got anywhere."

"No, no, dear. Now you know where you are going and that's half the battle. Now you know what to aim for, don't you?"

"But Mother, you can't stop temptation. I still look back—I still feel the past. Being as selfish as I am..."

"No, my dear. This is a grace, to look hard at yourself and see your faults."

"I have been so afraid, really," said Sister Mary Ruth Ann. "For such a long time I've looked at this profession as the beginning of my whole life and I kept finding faults, things that got in my way in getting this far. But now, as far as I'm concerned I might as well be taking my final vows."

"And you have no doubts?" said Mother Cyr, her voice soft but intense.

Sister Mary Ruth Ann's face suddenly blazed with joy. "No, Mother, no doubts," she answered.

"You are making a dedication. That's the right way to feel."

"That's why it has scared me so much. It's such a big thing, like going to the death chamber—dying tomorrow."

"No, no, dear—to be reborn again... You have the same grace as at baptism. But you know—let God do what he wants with you. When you make your vows, you put yourself at God's disposal. You are ready for anything—you are answering a call. I can only recommend that you be a child of God. If He wants you to serve Him in a significant way, fine—praise Him. But if it's small things, it makes no difference."

"I know, Mother. You once told me to sanctify everything I did—even polishing doorknobs. And it worked. Before that, maybe I felt too grown up to be a child of God. Oh, Mother, I owe so much—so much. May I have your blessing?"

"You have it, my dear. And you are at peace? No longer afraid?"

"Well, Mother—almost."

The next day, along with twenty-two other novices, Sister Mary Ruth Ann professed her vows to God in a simple ceremony. Still wearing their white veils, the novices filed into the church past their families—many of whom they had not seen for two and a half years. Each carried the black veil and crucifix to be added to her habit as a professed sister. Then all retired to the sanctuary, where, in silence, they dressed and adjusted the heavy Marist cross on a blue cord at their necks. Over a white peaked cap, a sign of their sisterhood's origins in France, they folded the heavy black veils of profession. Then all re-entered the church to kneel before the bishop.

In her hand each sister held a lighted candle bound with a small white ribbon and a sprig of orange blossom—symbol of her intention to burn out her life in God's service as one of Christ's brides. One by one they professed themselves as the bishop, crook in hand, moved in front of each sister to hear her pronounce her vows. Sister Mary Ruth Ann bit her lip nervously as the bishop approached. Then, in a voice little above a whisper, she spoke the three vows that bound her to God and the Marist Missionary family.

As soon as the ceremony was complete, the newly professed sisters filed out, to the excited greetings and embraces of their families. For Sister Mary Ruth Ann the moment was almost overwhelming. Her grandfather, his eyes filling with tears, rushed to her through the throng and clutched her silently. Neither was able to speak until finally the young sister said, " Grandfather, my hand shook so much I was sure my candle would go out. When my turn came, I could hardly find my voice. But I made it," she cried triumphantly. "I made it!" Her grandfather released her and for a moment studied her face, shining with joy and wet with tears. "Your mother," he said, "will call you at the convent tonight. She said she would come to see you in the late spring." Sister Mary Ruth Ann reached for his hand, biting her lip once more to hold back her tears.

All around them other grandparents, mothers, fathers, sisters, and brothers stood looking at the young sisters in awe. In some faces, sorrow mixed itself with pride. In others, there was only joy, for each girl carried the radiance of her great achievement like a halo of God's special love for her. Then all collected in the church hall to talk excitedly over the events of the day, the difficulties of the past, and their expectations for the future. Each young sister knew that for a while she would be sent to work in one of the local Marist convents, freeing an older sister to go to college or "out to the missions." By dealing with the ordinary things of this world, packing medical supplies for the far-flung Marist clinics and leprosariums, taxiing her superiors and sisters to college and meetings, ordering food and answering the telephones, attending to boilers and cooking meals and running the laundry, she would be drawn gently back from the refined realm of spirit into the practical world. When her readjustment to mundane things was complete, her superiors would send her, in her turn, to begin professional training aimed at equipping her for work in the missions. Those who had already completed college could expect to be returned to school for refresher courses. Those who had joined the Marists from high school would now begin study as undergraduates at a Catholic, secular, or state college.

At the end of the novitiate, each young sister had been asked by her superiors to choose three careers that interested her. If, after her time of readjustment to the world, she still felt inclined to the same careers and if her superiors thought her suited to those she had chosen, they would confer with her and prepare a plan in keeping with the missions' needs, the girl's skills, and the superiors' assessment of her abilities. The result would be practical training for some as teachers, some as nurses, some as social workers, a few as dentists and doctors and therapists. The only limitation the Marists would place upon her education would be that of geography; she would attend college near enough a Marist convent to commute to her campus from "home."

But today, college years and careers were only expectations. Today was a time to bask in their great spiritual achievement and to catch up with their families on news of those they had left behind in the world. Finally, the "brides" were called by Mother Mary Ambrose to return to the convent, where their sisters impatiently waited to greet them. Clutching presents from their families, they left for "home" and the praises and prayers of thanksgiving that awaited them. Later, there was a special private party of the sisterhood, complete with a bridal cake surmounted by lily of the valley and a small statue of the Blessed Mother, whose special spirit they had just vowed to follow for the rest of their lives.

The long struggle of the spirit was rewarded; the translation of that spirit into the work of hand and mind could now begin. In time, Sister Mary Ruth Ann learned from Mother Mary Ambrose that she would become a social worker for the Marists. In a few months she would be sent to college, and later, she would work in the Marist Missions to the poor —perhaps in Peru, where the need for trained specialists in social work was abundantly clear. "God's work in the world," a service of love and understanding, lay before the young sister, and her heart filled with joy at the prospect.

The period of the novitiate is really very short. The spiritual formation is so important that each day of these two years is precious. During the novitiate, the pendulum is swung completely to spirituality. Now, as the sister re-enters the world, the apostolic life looms large, and for a while it may become all-consuming. But with the years the spiritual side regains its balancing force and the two intertwine so that both sides of her express her love for God. She begins to grow in the depth of her understanding of life. From here on, just as in human love, divine love solidifies. She learns to be less emotional—to give and give, and to become happier in the giving.

PAGES

67   *At midmorning Examine, a time of self-scrutiny, a novice kneels in contemplation. During the first canonical year of the novitiate, all but an hour and a half of the day is spent in silence and study.*

68-69   *The intensity of their inner search for awareness of God shows in the faces of second-year novices during retreat before profession.*

70-71   *Sister Mary Ruth Ann searches for guidance in the Way of the Cross during her retreat.*

72-73   *The two-year trial of the novitiate is nearly over, and Sister Mary Ruth Ann answers her superior's questions in the final Canonical Examination. "No, Mother, I have no doubts."*

74-75   *In the last moments before first profession, second-year novices dress in black capes, the peaked caps of the Marist Society, and the black veil of professed sisters.*

76-77   *In the simple Profession Ceremony the new sisters recite prayers in common; then each takes her vow separately before the bishop. Her candle, bound with ribbon and orange blossom, signifies the intention of a "bride" to burn out her life in God's service.*

78-79   *A long struggle with loneliness ends when Sister Mary Ruth Ann greets her grandfather after profession.*
80   *Sister Mary Ruth Ann is thrilled to receive the news of her assignment to study social work from Mother Mary Ambrose. Mission work will follow college.*

81   *"Brides of Christ," bearing gifts from their families, return to embrace their sisters after profession.*

82   *Later, the youngest of the professed cuts a bridal cake at the convent party.*

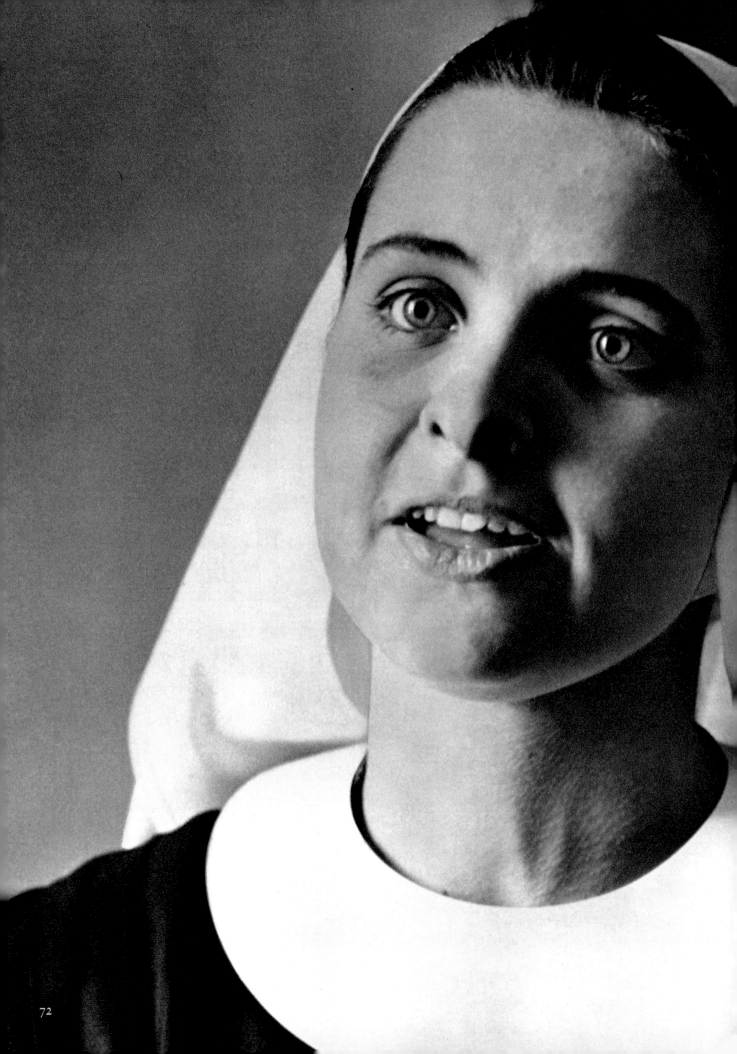

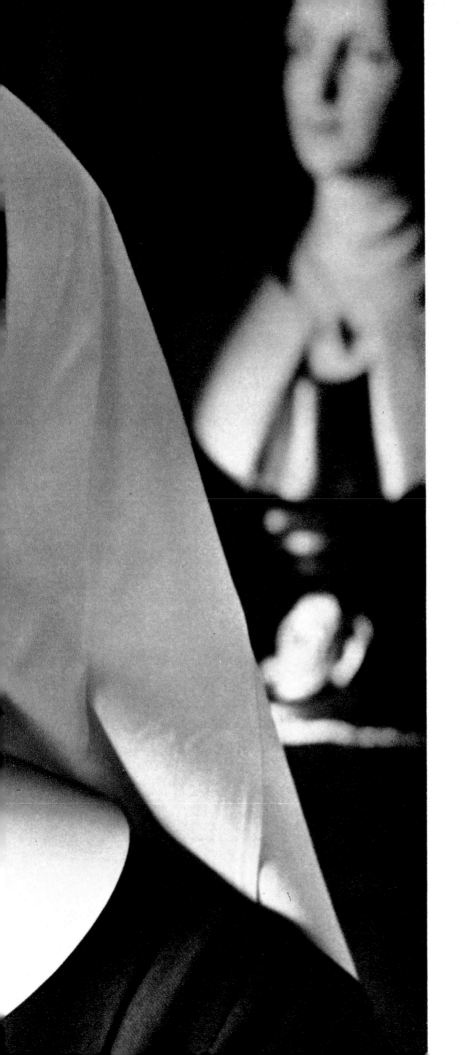

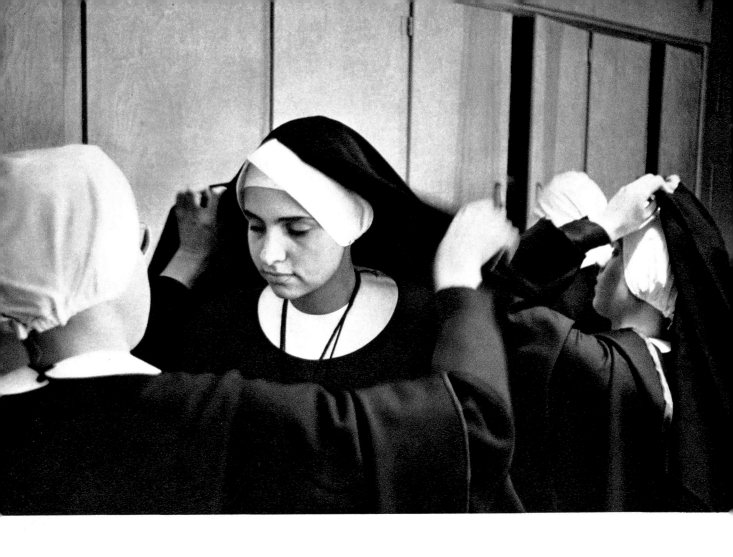

CHAPTER

IV

The years between profession and mission assignment are years of impatience, despite the absorbing business of being trained as a nurse, doctor, social worker, teacher, or secretary. The young professed sister feels that she lives between two worlds and is anxious to dispense with pure theory and test herself against reality in the missions. Sister Mary Jan, now professed and pursuing her studies, said, "Before, in the novitiate, we lived in an ideal world where everything was spirit. Now we've begun to practice living a little bit—to recommit ourselves to the world and be free. It's up to us to watch over our temptations, to rededicate ourselves each day and probe our thoughts and actions to be sure that we have done what God wished. You always find, as you review, evidence of His hand at work, evidence of His design, and in a way it makes you even more anxious to go forward. There is such dignity in bringing God to the world that all of us, espoused to Him, want to give ourselves totally. Love is like gold—it must be purified by the fires before it comes through. It takes everyday life—far beyond the ideals of the novitiate — to make you really grow. Waiting, you get to feel like a powerhouse of spirituality that must have an outlet! You can't quash it much longer, and oh, how much you want to get started with His work even if you are only the cook for the other sisters in a mission. It's really becoming imperative. Without sacrifice, how can you prove your love?"

In her years of training, the missionary has been taught that sacrifice is synonymous with love. She has learned to regard the simplicity and routine of convent life as an opportunity to demonstrate her love of God and to sanctify the smallest task, each privation of comfort, and the long hours of study and prayer in His name. Yet during these years she knows that her vocation has never been tried except by her own fears. In the convent she has lived untouched by outside strains, her days passing as predictably as beads on a rosary. She has not yet been really tested in her vocation in the outside world. Her vows, temporary for six years after first profession, are hedged by freedom; she will not meet any final test of vocation or profess herself perpetually until she is assigned to the missions.

"Strangely," said Mother Mary Ambrose, "it is just when a girl learns that sacrifice means love that God begins to withdraw some of His consolations. One of the first great consolations to be withdrawn when she completes her training is her own family. As soon as her study years are over she must accept separation from them for up to twelve years."

When a Marist sister is ready for mission, she makes a final visit home. During her two weeks of relative freedom she is touched once more by the world she has left behind. The familiar pictures of memory become reality again; here are the streets of childhood, the school friends, the room that was once her own. She sees unmistakably the sadness that is masked behind her parents' smiles and realizes that the long separation demanded by her mission will cost them as much pain as any privation she will face. She must also admit that time is watching from the shadows; this could be a final farewell. Age and death await those she loves, perhaps while she is far away. The last week home becomes a trial of love. With those who have given her life she must gather and give what she can in one week to sustain years apart. The rest, she must believe, is "in the hands of God."

For Sister Mary Patricius, the last visit home was especially poignant. Her mother and father had given three daughters to religious life; only their son had married and remained close to them. Sister Mary Patricius was their youngest. When she left on mission to the slums of Lima, Peru, a large portion of life would be finished for them. The great gift of faith and sacrifice in the rearing and loving of three daughters would be over.

The week at home was filled with the occupations families use to protect themselves from the thought of imminent separation. "Things" must be bought for the mission—nursing bottles, blankets, baby scales. "Perhaps," Patrick Byrne asked his daughter, "you'd be needing a little brandy for medicinal purposes?" A family picnic, swarming with small nieces, nephews, and cousins, reminded Sister Mary Patricius forcefully of how long she would be away. To a child of ten she said, "You'll be grown and married when I come home."

The next day Patrick and Catherine Byrne drove their daughter back to the convent for the formal farewell. Five sisters were going out—Sister Mary Patricius and Sister Mary Thomas More, a physician, to a new medical mission in Lima, another sister to the leprosarium run by the Marist sisters in Jamaica, and two others to the "bush mission" of the far South Pacific. Most of the younger sisters could expect to follow one of these new missionaries soon. No matter where they were sent, all would remain part of the circle of the sisterhood, secure in the sense of a community life of prayer and work that bound them together without regard for their location.

This unity in the sisterhood only emphasized the rending of the bonds that held together Sister Mary Patricius's own family. The next day at the airport she saw the hollows of sacrifice in her mother's face. "It was so hard to leave them," she recalled later in Lima, "almost unbearable in human terms. You wonder if you'll ever see them again; you can't help it. But then you realize God has asked, 'Lovest thou Me more than these?' That's what He asked when He first called you. Now you have the opportunity to answer.... When I got on the plane I felt terrible. I prayed, and finally He let me see what a gift I was given by this chance to serve where I was needed. Such a gift must cost something."

Such a gift did cost something. The courage to regard it as a grace had been learned from another heart. As the great plane bearing Sister Mary Patricius and Sister Mary Thomas More lifted on its thrust of jet and set its nose southward, Catherine Byrne stood at the airport window watching. Tears streamed down her cheeks while she clutched a tissue to her lips to stifle sound. Then as the plane faded to nothing in the vast blue of the sky, her head lifted, and somewhere in her grief she found pride that God had chosen her to serve Him thus.

The plane that carried the two nuns southward was taking them to a world violently different from the one they left behind. Both Sister Mary Patricius and Sister Mary Thomas More had followed religious life out of spiritual necessity. "They were called to a life of perfection," Mother Mary Ambrose had said. "A life above nature." This call to a supernatural life was now to be tested by reality in Mendocita, one of the death-haunted slums in the suburbs called *barriadas* that form a "cincture of misery" around Lima.

Mary Byrne had never questioned where her vocation would lead. Her call to mission life had come just after completion of high school. Obediently she had followed it, joyfully accepting the decision of her superiors that she be trained as a nurse. She had graduated first in her nursing class from St. Vincent's hospital near Boston and was now to be a nurse at the Marists' new medical clinic for the poor in Mendocita.

Sister Mary Thomas More, formerly Beth O'Brien, had decided to enter the Marist Society when she was a senior at Fordham University, completing premedical studies. "My brother wondered why I didn't wait for my shoe salesman to come along," she said, "but I knew this was what I wanted. I gave up medicine to enter the convent. I didn't believe I could go on with it. But I felt the most important half of my life was missing if I did not enter—the spiritual half."

The Marists had trained her spiritually and then promptly returned her to her medical studies. These years were followed by a rigorous internship at the largest public hospital in New York City, where she worked the night emergency ward side by side with the men who were her colleagues. "I would get so tired," she recalled, "but I kept the Rule and completed the office every day somehow. Without prayer, life was incomplete."

The emergency ward taught her about life as few ever see it. It prepared and toughened her for the trials she was to face in Peru. In the last year, she had finished those preparations by earning a master's degree in public health at Harvard University—a year's study added to all the other years, at her own request, when a trip to Lima in preparation for opening the clinic had revealed to her the scope of the problems that lay ahead. She now approached those problems as coolly as a general on the eve of a great and costly battle. She did not know exactly what the future held, but she was ready for it.

Sister Mary Patricius did not have the same degree of preparation and could not anticipate what lay ahead. She would find herself severely tested by the suffering she was to witness and by the knowledge that beyond the circle of her own work poverty lay like a bottomless sea, utterly unconquerable.

Mendocita, where the clinic was located, was one of the oldest *barriadas*. Many of its inhabitants were second-generation slum dwellers, full of bitterness, hostile to outsiders and suspicious of *gringos* even when they were dressed as priests or nuns. It had the squalor of an old slum despite the fact that it enjoyed "improvements" such as electricity, water, and regularly laid out streets. Over the years the streets had become little more than mud ruts running with water from the open taps, each of which supplied about eighty families. The water was impure. The main street was full of garbage. As there were no provisions for sanitary needs, the stench in Mendocita was inescapable. Rats inhabited the adobe shacks with the people who crowded together eight and ten to a room. Wherever the sisters went on their inspection of health conditions, they found subhuman circumstances. They also found children. The missions to the slums over the last years had provided just enough food in the form of American surplus aid to keep alive many children who might otherwise have died. The population of the *barriadas* was increasing and the poverty deepening.

For Sister Mary Patricius the transition from the plenty of North America and the convent's private world to the harsh terms of life in Mendocita was overwhelming. The stream of children who were brought to the clinic suffering from malnutrition, their stomachs swollen and eyes beseeching, enlarged her sense of helplessness. She learned from a Maryknoll sister at the Lima Mission, the coordinating headquarters for twenty foreign missions at work in the slums, that these children "can expect eleven glasses of milk and fourteen pounds of meat a year—if they are lucky. Half of the people live on fifteen hundred calories a day—just half the minimum daily requirement." At work in the clinic she heard a Peruvian doctor who volunteered his services once a week say, "Look at this child; these are the beginnings of TB. The cause? Poverty, the culture of the *pueblo*, the infection lurking there all the time. They have no meat, no fish, no milk. The baby lives on tea. His father, a carpenter, can find only a half day's work. He earns forty *soles* [$1.50] a week—and on that he must feed his wife and two children."

Sister Mary Patricius knew, as she administered an injection the doctor had ordered for a little boy, that it would alleviate only part of his affliction. Treatment might prevent him from contracting TB, but hunger still stalked him and, with it, other illnesses. Even the task at hand was complicated. She could not tell his mother that her little Juan should have pills every four hours until his fever subsided. Her Spanish lessons, taken in the United States, were almost useless to communicate with her Indian patients, most of whom spoke a polyglot of Quechua— the ancient language of the Incas—and Spanish. "Even if I could make her understand," she asked, "how will she know when four hours pass? If there were a clock, she couldn't read it." Sister Mary Patricius also knew that it was possible that the pills given for Juan that morning would be sold for a few pennies by evening. There was need for food in his home.

No American training could have prepared her for these frustrations or for the wave of helplessness and guilt that overtook her. She reacted by becoming ill. She was cold all the time.

Her hands shook. She lost all appetite and could not sleep. The comfort she and her sisters had enjoyed at the Marist convent in a wealthy suburb seemed to her a mockery of the misery of her patients. In her heart she knew she faced the real test of her vocation for the first time.

"Our Father Who art in Heaven, hallowed be Thy name, Thy kingdom come, Thy will be done on earth as it is in heaven...." God's will, unfathomable and all-encompassing, had brought her here. The suffering she saw, though humanly incomprehensible, was part of His plan. "Glory be to the Father and to the Son and to the Holy Spirit...." Where was His glory? Sister Mary Patricius turned to her rosary—the heavy beads she had received as a novice in that faraway world of the convent where the life of pure spirit had filled her with sweet serenity. In daily prayer—in thought of the Virgin Mary, "blessed amongst women," "full of grace," and of her Son walking His bloody way to Calvary beneath his heavy cross, living His agony and dying for all mankind, she found guidance. For suffering had been the way of Christ—and the suffering she saw surely must be part of His plan. "Thy will be done," she prayed, "on earth as it is in heaven...."

"I needed all the help prayer could give," she reflected later. "Somehow keeping the Rule, hanging on to its familiar routine, I got through those first weeks." In a few months she learned to accept the terms of her mission. She did not look for hope, except in prayer. She did not expect solutions except those beyond her understanding. She simply worked against the overwhelming odds and took joy in small victories. Little Juan recovered. The children on the streets of Mendocita were coming to know her. "*Madrecita*," they called out when she walked through the alleyways—"Little mother." "You come to see God shining through everything," she said, "and you are at peace."

Sister Mary Jogues, the Marist superior at the mission convent in Peru, commented, "An American girl just can't learn to be a missionary until she is one. She must learn from God's hands. A missionary vocation today requires a great deal of stability and maturity; the girls don't come in with this—it's something that our training and work have to teach them. It doesn't come in two years, but gradually, with suffering and experience. The greatest suffering lies in witnessing the pain of others and knowing you are helpless to do all that should be done." Faced with the reality of poverty that afflicts the majority of the world's people, the missionary sister loses her youthful sense of heroism. She stops thinking of herself as someone who can help, and thus sheds the last shred of condescension and superiority. "She becomes one with the people," said Sister Mary Jogues. "Their pain is her pain, their need her need. She becomes more patient, more tolerant this way, closer to a true mission spirit. With the help of her contact with God, her certainty grows. She has peace, and that peace radiates to those among whom she lives and works. She cares for them with openness of heart, and this may cause them to wonder and ask where her strength comes from. They may begin to search for the source of peace that shines through her life. She does not need to proselytize."

Sister Mary Thomas More's reaction to Mendocita was different. She could not permit herself to feel helpless, though she did admit once, "I feel like someone with her finger in the dike." The seemingly insuperable task before her became a challenge to be organized and broken into conquerable parts. One part was medical, one part social, one part political, one part a problem of education. She knew, though, that the whole was larger than these parts—that Mendocita was a microcosm of the griefs of a nation and a continent.

"We must first give these people a sense of their own dignity," she said, describing the work to which she intended to devote her life. "This is not just a question of giving them medical help or handing out food on a bread line. It is not simply a health problem over-all, but a human problem. To give these people a chance to live as human beings, we will have to use every ounce of good will and every bit of help we can get. All the missions and all the Peruvian agencies must work together to give these people a chance to pull themselves up."

She began by taking and passing five separate medical examinations in Spanish to qualify herself for a Peruvian license to practice. She then contacted Peruvian doctors specializing in everything from obstetrics to respiratory illnesses and asked them to spend volunteer time in her clinic. She began a full-scale medical survey of Mendocita, consulting the Lima Mission to coordinate her findings with the conditions that prevailed in other *barriadas*. She met with the lay brothers who were doctors and traveled with their mobile clinic to outlying villages. From the Saint James fathers, who had established Parroquia San Ricardo Mission, where her clinic was, she learned which families in Mendocita might form the core of an adult education program on food, nutrition, and hygiene. She ran her clinic daily as well, seeing patients whose illnesses ranged from venereal disease to psychosis. Finally, when the path of her own future in Mendocita was mapped, she looked to the task that would confront the Marist sisters who would follow her to Peru. She was ready for a trip to the mountains.

From Cuzco, the ancient capital of the Incas lying at eleven thousand feet in the Andes, a road winds northward to Lima, following a route charted long ago by the runners of the Inca emperors. A trip by truck from Cuzco to Lima takes many days; the Inca relay runners had supplied fresh fish brought from the sea to the palaces of the mountain kings in one day. It is a road into a timeless land where life is little changed from the time when the conquistadors divided the Inca empire into demesnes for the bold Spanish adventurers. The *haciendas* remain vast feudal holdings where Indian families live virtually as serfs. There is little hope in these mountains, and it is the vainness of hope that has sent thousands down to the dank squalor of such *barriadas* as Mendocita. Most of those who remain are empty of dreams, as patient as stones.

Sister Mary Thomas More and Sister Mary Patricius started from Cuzco at dawn on a trip into the future mission field of the Marist sisters. The road became a white dust ribbon as it wound higher and higher into the Andean fastness. At sixteen thousand feet the air became so thin that it burned the eyes. The Apurímac River lay far below, and what were fabled to be the ruins of the bridge of San Luis Rey stood as a mute monument to other travelers lost in time. Small crosses were planted in the side of the road where some of those who had more recently come this way had been lost. In the pool of crystalline air below the truck windows a hawk hung in an updraft like some winged fish. It was a road to be prayed over. The two sisters sat bouncing in the truck and silently read their office. Most of their days in Mendocita were spent in prayer of the hands—their work with the sick and poor given as an offering of love for Him and His.

But in the silence of this ancient and majestic land the haunting psalms of the Hours brought a special refreshment, for the mountains seemed to fold His mighty power in their terrible heights. "Let them discourse on the glory of your kingdom and speak of your might.... Your kingdom is a kingdom for all ages and your dominion endures through all generations...."

One afternoon they stopped at a village founded by the Incas called Limatambo—"resting place by the lime tree." Children swarmed around them, their hands quarreling for the brightly colored "holy cards" which Sister Mary Patricius distributed. Their eager eyes told the doctor of fever, and she examined the town's water supply, one pump perpetually flowing into the village square. "You can practically see the animals in it," she remarked to the Saint James father who had driven them there and who called the village home. He told her that dysentery and fever were omnipresent in his parish, "about three hundred square miles without anything but mule track across it." The local health officer had little more than a sixth-grade education and the nearest doctor was at least a half day away from Limatambo by truck—a week away from most of the villages that lay in the mountains. The American priest looked at the sister doctor and asked in Spanish "*¿Le gusta, Madre?*" (Do you like it, Mother?). "*Sí, Padre,*" she replied emphatically, "*This* is mission."

The sisters were silent after the truck left Limatambo and ground onward into the mountains. The powder of the road filtered past the window seals and settled in ghostly streaks on their black habits. Passing from one valley to another they learned from the American priest who drove them that "Every valley is a *hacienda* for cattle with twenty or thirty Indian families taking care of them. In return for their work they receive a very small wage. They may plant a little corn and live on the land, but if they should ever save enough to own a cow they must pay rent to graze it, and within a few years they find they don't own the cow any more. She has been forfeited for overdue rent. That's why in Curahuasi, where we are heading, we have started a cooperative, using church lands. We are trying to teach them how to raise better maize crops—but also how to raise other good food crops. We are up to our ears in chickens at the moment because we can teach them how to raise hens for eggs instead of the pot. We don't expect to make them understand owning these chickens or a share in the land overnight— since they've never really owned anything before. It's a slow process of education." Then he added, "Patience isn't a virtue here. It's something that is forced on you." "It must be a hard thing, father," the doctor sister answered thoughtfully, "to make your gait meet theirs."

Later that afternoon, when the truck dropped down into the valley where Curahuasi lay, she was to walk a way with the people of this village and listen to the rhythms to which their gait was paced. The first sound she heard when the truck stopped in front of the church was the knelling of the death bell. Mourners were huddled around a coffin and another priest from the United States, Father John Mee, was completing the funeral service on the steps of the church. Behind him in the darkness an altar lamp flickered before the place where God sat—but the Indians, afraid that death might contaminate this holy place, would not bring the coffin inside.

Within the frail plank box, which was painted orange, lay the body of a twenty-year-old boy. His name had been Placito; he was the youngest son and only support of his mother. As the mourners lifted the coffin and began to walk toward the cemetery, she walked behind him, weeping and talking to herself. The wind blew unceasingly, the blue gum trees moving, the air filled with their fragrance and with the rich licorice smell of newly cut anisette. The wind roared in the hollow shell of the valley, distorting the women's sobs and bringing close the laughter of children across the village. The mountains loomed brown and purple, vast and far-reaching toward the thin blue of the sky. The death bell sounded again, a rattle of metal catching inside the bell before each toll as the mourners, many of them barefooted, walked to the cemetery over a pale gray road which was full of little stones.

At the graveside, Father Mee said the final prayers. Placito's sister bent over the coffin to look through a crack at his face. Then the orange box was lowered, its sides scratching against the stony earth. The women began to keen, one voice lifting to tell a remembered tale of Placito's life as another dropped in weeping. The birds called on the windy air and the earth fell with a thumping sound on the orange box. A woman with a baby on her back turned from the keening to pick up the remains of a dried wreath from a grave nearby.

"You come up here three or four times a week and the human sorrow of it touches you," said Father Mee, "but you begin to wonder, with a life like this, hungry, half drunk to keep going...maybe death is a blessing. And look at it," he said, his arm gesturing toward the towering Andes. "Isn't it beautiful up here? The day before yesterday I buried a twenty-two-year-old girl, the mother of three. This morning a baby boy. This afternoon a mother brought another one in dying. I held it—I gave it what I could. An hour later the father was back. The baby was dead."

The keening for Placito continued until his short life was reviewed. Memory released the family's pain; the stories seemed to make him live again as the earth was methodically dropped to cover the orange box in which the boy lay.

As they walked back to the village Father Mee said, "Sisters, these people get just enough food to stay alive if they do nothing but lie in bed all day. But they are up working, carrying tremendous packs on their backs up and down these mountains. Think of what that does; they burn themselves up. Their lives might discourage you, make you feel defeated—until you see how much just a little can do."

"This is mission country, Father," the two replied, and then Sister Mary Thomas More said, "If I could only come up here once a month to screen and plan things, perhaps I could begin to help right away."

In the village a small crowd had already gathered at the priests' dispensary. Word of this strange *gringo* sister who was a doctor had spread, and when Sister Mary Thomas More entered the small room she found the sick leaning patiently against the walls. Unnamed fever raged behind the beautifully boned faces and gave a dark burning luster to their eyes. The air was filled with the choked sobbing of children whose lungs were congested and bodies frail. "I feel," the doctor muttered, recalling her words in Mendocita, "like someone with a finger in the dike, but the water is coming over anyway."

Before attending any patients she looked through the stock of drugs the priests had on their shelves. They were the contribution of countless doctors' offices in the United States — samples of the new drugs to control the ills of a rich nation. There were tranquillizers, sleeping pills, tonics for the tired, medication for overstrained hearts. There was little that could be used for the diseases of poverty except the antibiotics, which were in shortest supply.

The doctor's first patient was a child who was wearing a beautifully knit hat. Bright dancing figures ran in rings around the hat; they seemed to hold hands. The baby's head rolled weakly on his mother's breast as he gasped for breath. When the mother looked up into the doctor's face, Father Mee stepped forward. "But that baby…" he began. He bent quickly over the mother and child and then turned to the father, who stood silently beside the woman. "Your other son?" he asked, his voice just above a whisper. The man nodded, his gentle face strained with sadness. "Father," he said, "I want the bells for my son—but I cannot pay for them. I will work for you instead." The priest touched his hands and said, "You shall have the bells. There is no cost." Then he turned back to the sisters. "It was his other child—the twin to this one—that died this afternoon."

The doctor found that this baby was also gravely ill. The cause was a raging tubercular fever in the mother that had infected her milk. The doctor ordered that the child be transferred to an aunt who was also nursing and told Father Mee what course of treatment to follow for both mother and child. The first dosage was administered immediately in hope of saving the dying child.

When night came down on the sierra the tired doctor and nurse climbed into another truck to continue their journey. They had listened for the first time to the slow heartbeat of the mountains, to the unceasing wind from the empty heights, the ringing of the death bell, the patient shuffling of feet along the pale stony camino that now they followed into the darkness. It was late—near the last of the Hours and the night prayer of Compline: "For He knows how we are formed; he remembers that we are dust. Man's days are like those of grass; like a flower of the field he blooms; the wind sweeps over him and he is gone and his place knows him no more.…" Tomorrow they would return to Curahuasi to see the funeral of the dead twin begin its journey over this same road to the cemetery where they had left Placito. But there would have been one small human victory over the immense forces that decreed death in this empty mountain land; the second twin would live. The sisters did not know this as the truck ground upward into the velvet black night full of stars. The mountain passes were cloaked in absolute darkness and the camino seemed a ghostly road warily winding its way higher and higher into a vast emptiness. It was a long, long way until dawn, when they would hear mass and bow their heads to delicate chimes as the Host was lifted heavenward.

PAGES

93   *A traditional farewell ceremony is held for the sisters who will depart for the missions after taking home leave.*

94–95   *Now at home, Sister Mary Patricius plays with her nieces and nephews at a picnic.*

96–97   *Sister Mary Patricius kisses her mother good-by at the airport. (Far right:) Watching the plane ready for takeoff, Mrs. Byrne stands weeping, with another daughter, a Dominican nun.*

98–99   *As the plane thrusts skyward, Mrs. Byrne lifts her face in a moment of grief, pride, and joy.*

100–101   *In the San Ricardo Mission nursing Sister Mary Patricius finds poverty and disease awaiting her. (Top right:) Juan receives antibiotics for his incipient tuberculosis.*

102–103   *Each morning after mass, San Ricardo Mission distributes bread and milk to the poor.*

104–105   *(Bottom:) Sister Mary Patricius laughs with two of the children. (Right:) Five-year-old Celestrina has just received two loaves and milk. Such children helped Sister Mary Patricius in a dark time.*

106   *During a health survey of Mendocita, Sister Mary Patricius and Sister Mary Thomas More talk with children.*

107   *The Marist cross finds admiring eyes in Mendocita. (Bottom:) In the Andean village of Limatambo during a trip into future mission country, Sister Mary Patricius distributes Sacred Heart cards.*

108–109   *The hands of the faithful reach for the holy cards.*

110–112   *In Curahuasi, high in the Andean mountains, the sisters arrive to see the funeral of Placito, a twenty-year-old boy.*

113   *Placito's sister takes a last look at his face through the coffin's cracked cover.*

114–115   *As Father John Mee reads the final prayers, Placito's mother touches the coffin and begins to keen.*

116–117   *In the clinic of the Saint James priests, Sister Mary Thomas More found patients waiting. Here she listens to the symptoms being described.*

118   *The nun physician advises a father on treatment for his child, infected by his tubercular mother.*

119   *Sister Mary Thomas More listens for sounds of chest congestion in another child with suspected tuberculosis.*

120–123   *In Abancay, the doctor and nurse kneel for mass. Dawn lifts the mist from the Andes.*

124   *Although they can help only a few today, the Marists look to the future for the fruition of their work.*

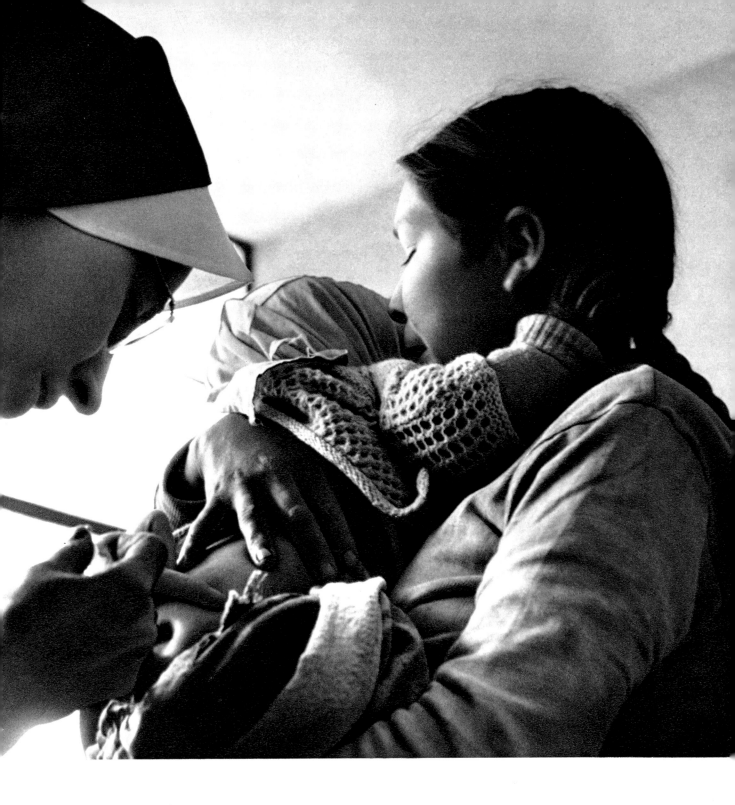

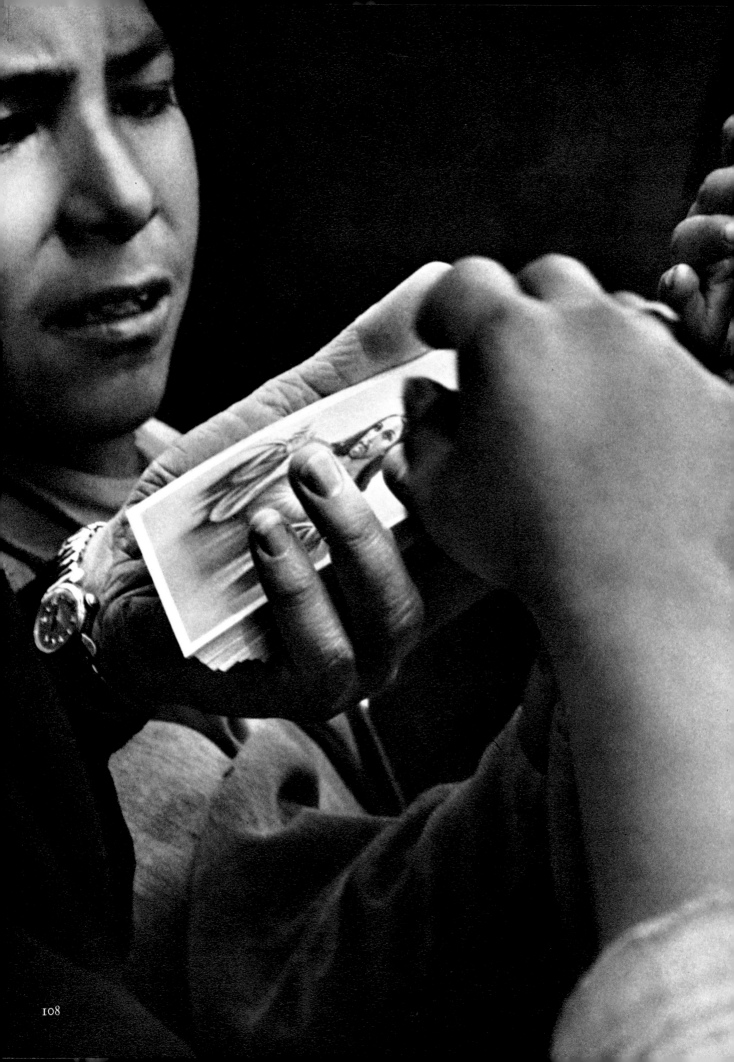

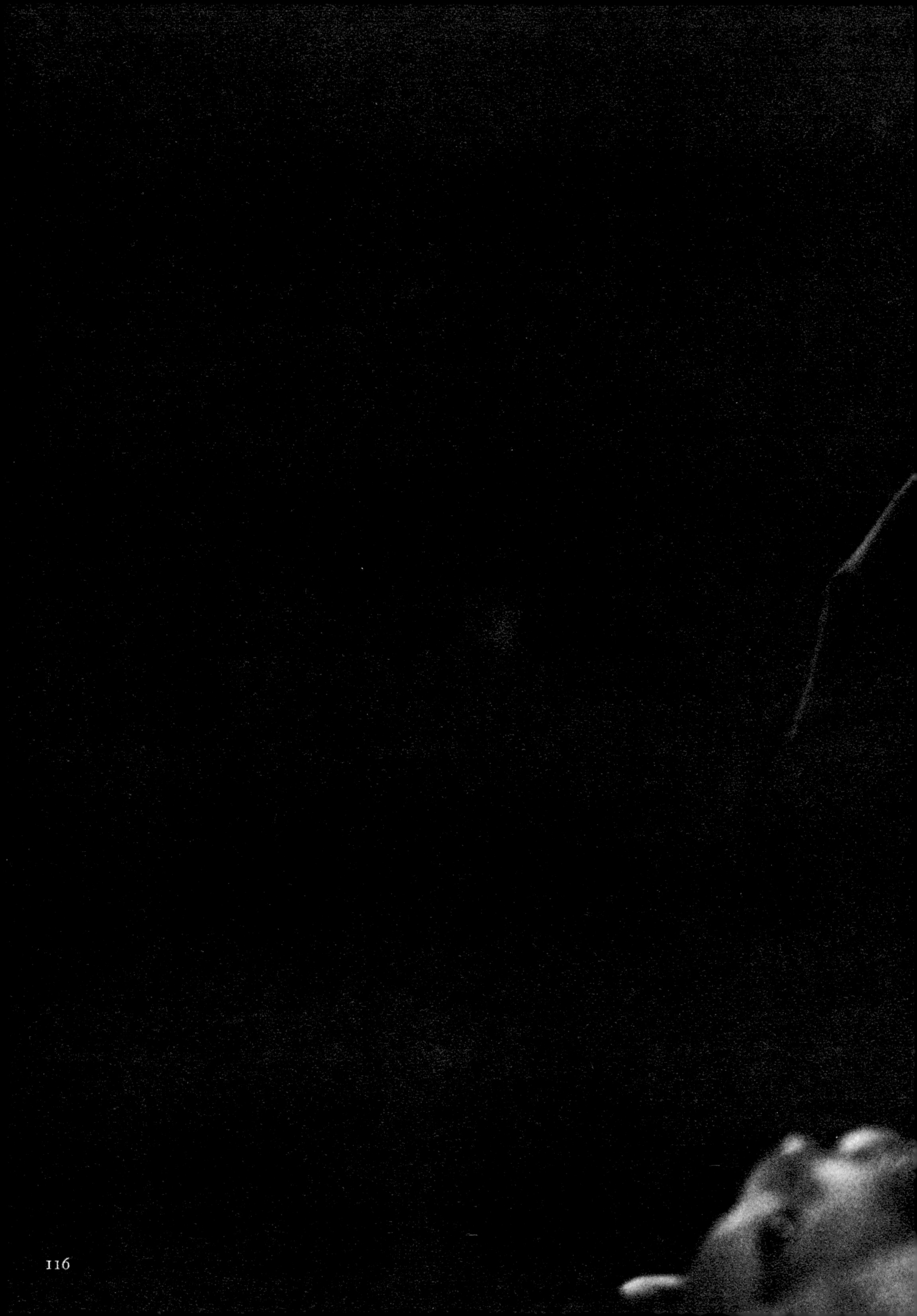

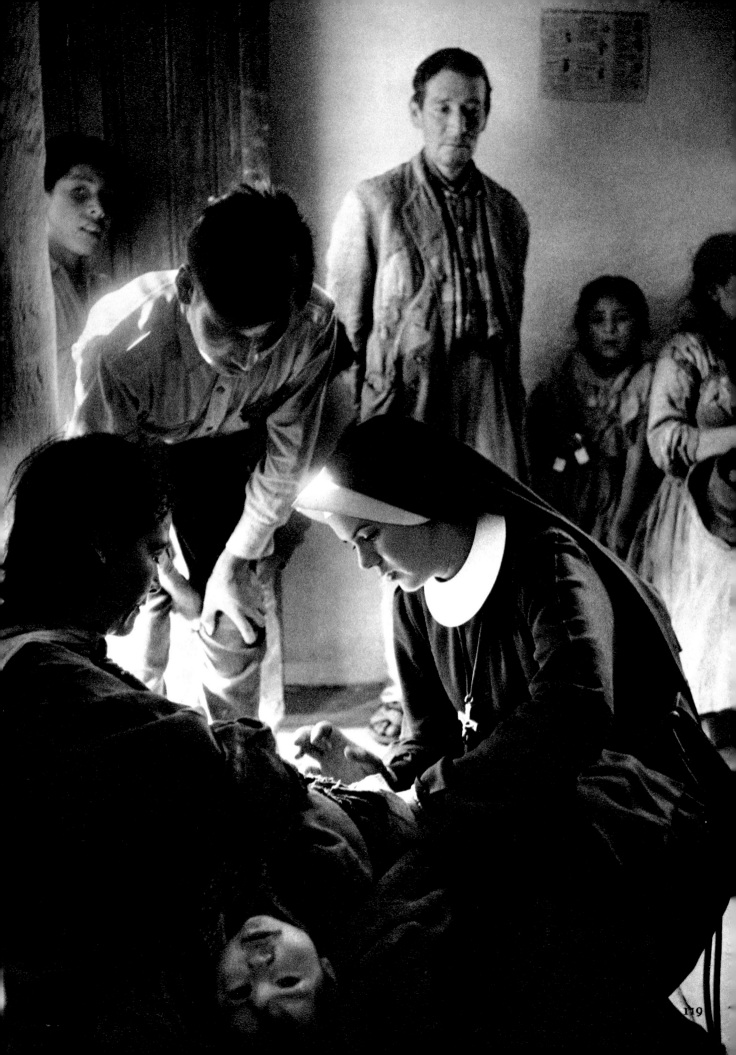